sisters understand each other because they share the same roots

pictures and verse
by
Sandra Magsamen

gift

stewart tabori & chang

There is
no one in
the world
like you.

You are my friend

and my
sister
too.

You know
the history and
stories of where
our lives come
from.

Together
we share
precious
memories of
the past...

and
delight in
whatever
may come.

You
are wise,
honest
and true.

I value
Your advice
and
opinions

and thank
you for always
being there
to speak to.

I trust
and count
on you with
all my
heart...

even though
we sometimes
disagree,
nothing could
keep us apart.

Your smile
and laughter
are a
comfort to me,

only you
understand
what is
so very
funny.

I love you
for caring
and
believing
in me.

I am
grateful
we grow from
the same
family tree.

Pictures and verse by Sandra Magsamen
© 2001 Hanny Girl Productions, Inc.

Published in 2001 by
Stewart, Tabori & Chang
A division of Harry N. Abrams, Inc.
115 West 18th Street
New York, NY 10011

Distributed in Canada by
General Publishing Company Ltd.
30 Lesmill Road
Don Mills, Ontario, Canada M3B2J6

ISBN: 1-58479-069-5

Printed in Hong Kong

10 9 8 7 6 5 4 3 2 1

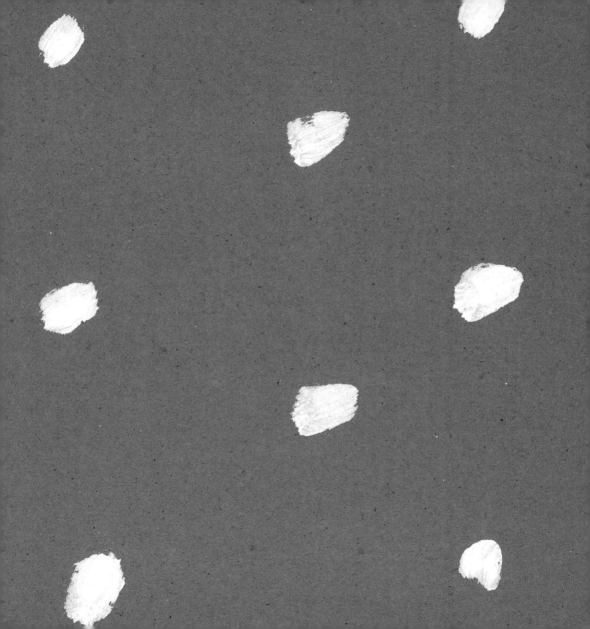